THE
DAD
EDGE
TRACKER

THE DAD EDGE ALLIANCE

HEALTH

FINANCES

RELATIONSHIP

CHILDREN

BUSINESS

WILDLY IMPORTANT GOALS

TABLE OF CONTENTS

DEDICATION

This journal/action plan is dedicated to fathers who feel a burning desire to step up their game in the six areas. Before we get to what this journal will help you execute in your life, let's first explain your current state and why you have this journal.

You have decided to take a step forward and take massive action in your life. Most men will live a quiet life of desperation taking their dreams and the life they wanted to live to their grave.

Most men live alone and isolated. We are physically surrounded by people, yet mentally, emotionally, and spiritual we are going at life alone.

Isolation is the enemy of excellence and no man ever achieved greatness on his own.

Living an intentional productive life of excellence takes structure, accountability, setting relevant achievable goals, and relentless execution.

Most men are in what we call "THE GRIND." We get up. We shower. We get our cup of coffee. We see our kids for 15 minutes (if we are lucky). We drive to a job we hate for a paycheck to support family we don't see much and when we do, we are usually too exhausted and burnt out to enjoy it. We come home. We see our wives and kids for a couple of hours. We watch the same TV shows. We go to bed. Get up the next day…wash…rinse…repeat.

This is the life of most men. On top of all that, we do this all alone.

The Dad Edge ALLIANCE
(THE BROTHERHOOD)

However, you have decided a different path. You have decided your life will now be different. You have joined a band of brothers called The Dad Edge Alliance who will help you along with your journey.

Men who are a part of the Alliance are HUNGRY. They are hungry to lead not just a good life, but a great, intentional, and purposeful life.

We are dedicated to being the best versions of ourselves. We desire to be inspired. We desire to learn. We desire to grow. We desire to live life full tilt and enjoy every minute possible.

THE PIT

That's not to say there won't be valleys while we are trying to climb the peaks. There absolutely will be valleys. In fact, at times the valley will turn into a pit. Every man takes their time and season in the pit.

The Pit is a period of time when men are challenged to the point of crumbling. Men will spend time in the PIT during times of divorce, death of a loved one, financial distress, lost connection and intimacy with a spouse, lost connection with a child, loss of a job, or even a health crisis.

It's important to realize that being in the pit doesn't make us less of the men we are. In fact, being in **the pit is a part of our journey through life.** If we weren't faced with challenges and adversity, how could we become stronger?

THE ROPE TEAM

Every man needs a rope team in their lives. No man will ever summit the top of Everest without a team behind them, in front of them, and even walking side by side.

The same holds true for life itself. Life is no different than climbing a mountain. There will be times when *we need* support, encouragement, and inspiration when we get weary. There will also be times when *we need to* support, encourage, and inspire others around us when they get weary. **The Alliance is our rope team.** When life gets difficult, our rope team is there to help us up.

OUR JOBS WITHIN THE ROPE TEAM

Everyone on our rope team has a job. Everyone in the Alliance has a responsibility to do two things:

- Ask for help when you need it
- When someone asks for help, support that man and throw him a rope.

We all realize how simple this sounds. However, **asking for help is the most difficult thing we do as men.** When we ask for help we feel weak. We feel it's a strike against us that we cannot handle what life throws at us. We feel inferior. We feel like an absolute loser.

LEANING IN

Gentlemen let's clear the air on this here and now. Asking for help is the most powerful thing you can do.

Here's why...when we ask for help, two things happen.

First, when we ask for help, there are plenty of men who feel honored knowing they are supporting you and helping you. **Being significant is one of the six basic human needs and men thrive on significance.** So, the next time you feel fearful or shame asking for help, understand that there are men waiting for an opportunity to make a difference in another man's life.

Second, when you ask for help, you inspire courage and strength for other men to raise their hands and ask for help. There are so many men that live in the shadows of fear and yearning for a helping hand.

When they see one man ask for help, it inspires the rest of us to take action, lean in, and ask for help.

THE 6 DIMENSIONS OF MEN/FATHERS

To fully understand how we can transform our lives, we first must understand how we operate as men and fathers. Men operate in six dimensions:

1. Our Health (Physical, Mental/Emotional, and Spiritual)
2. Financial (Our income, debt, stress, and emotional ties to money)
3. Relationship with our Wives
4. Relationship with our Kids
5. Business (How We Provide/What We Do for a Living)
6. W.I.G. (Wildly Important Goals)

HEALTH

When we think of "health" most of us automatically think of our physical health. However, there are 2 other critical dimensions to health.

Physical: Our physical bodies play a big role in how we function and how we even feel emotionally. Our bodies are our temple. By **taking care of the outside, it has a direct impact on internal wellbeing**.

Emotional/Mental: When most men think of emotions, we think of "airy-fairy, touchy-feely, sensitive nonsense." Nothing is further from the truth. As human beings, we are nothing more than a constant conversation with ourselves. Our emotions will rise up during these internal conversations. We can try to ignore them and even be successful for a short period of time. However, over time, the emotion will win and come out eventually. The more we repress our emotions, the more problems we will eventually have. **Our emotional health plays a critical role in our success**, relationships, productivity, and even enjoyment of life.

Spiritual: Our spiritual health is the relationship we have with God or our higher power. Spiritual health can mean different things to different men.

FINANCES

Finances play a very big role in our lives as men. **Finances actually impacts the other 4 dimensions of our lives.** It will impact our health, our relationships, and even what we decide to do for a living. Financial distress is also the culprit of 50% of all divorces.

In the Alliance, you will have access to several resources to help you: pay down debt, reduce your financial stress, have improved conversations with your spouse about money, create streams of revenue, and even businesses.

RELATIONSHIP WITH OUR WIVES

The relationship with our wives is the one of the most important relationships in our life. The majority of men report their marriage satisfaction to be average or slightly below average.

Believe it or not, **the relationship with your wife can thrive.**

In the Alliance, we spend a lot of time-sharing different ways and insights on how we can improve our relationships and make them thrive once again. It all comes down to: never getting complacent, always pursuing her, never stop dating her, and loving her in her love language.

Since the inception of the Alliance, I have seen relationships turn around even after divorce papers were on the lawyer's desk.

RELATIONSHIP WITH OUR KIDS

The relationship dynamics of with our kids is very different compared to the relationship with our wives. **Men desperately want to connect and have a strong bond with our kids.** However, most of us were not taught how to do this. We are simply making it up as we go and learning it on the fly.

In the Alliance, you will learn new and effective ways to connect with your kids and create an unbreakable bond. You will also learn ways to teach life lessons and share epic experiences.

WHAT WE DO FOR A LIVING

What we do for a living is a critical area of any man's life for several reasons. **Most men find a great deal of fulfillment, validation, and satisfaction in what we do to provide for our families.**

However, the opposite is also true for us. We can find ourselves hating our professional lives. We go to a job simply for the paycheck but hate what we do for a living. This can wreak havoc on our sleep, relationships, feelings of significance, contribution, self-worth, and even our health.

Finding out what we want to do for a living can be answered with one question: "What is the work I do that makes me come alive?"

We all have had times in our lives when we have done work that has made our mental, emotional, and professional being come alive. It's the feeling of the stars aligning and when work doesn't feel like "work."

So, let's explore this question...

WHAT WORK MAKES YOU COME *ALIVE*?

Once we answer this question, it now becomes extremely important to explore is, "What problems can you solve for someone?" Keep in mind, **you not only need to find the work that you love, but it also has to be valuable and solve a problem for someone else.**

If what you offer solves legitimate problems for someone else, now you are on to something.

The third and final step is creating a strategic plan. Most entrepreneurs fail at launching a business because they try to create it on shear drive and passion alone. Don't get me wrong, drive and passion are critical to your mission. Drive and passion are the fuel but are not the plan.

To get started, your plan should start with the following questions:

- **What unique skills do I have?**
- **What do I love doing?**
- **Why do I want to do it?**
- **Whose problem will I solve?**
- **How will I do it?**
- **When will I do it?**

Keep in mind, these questions will get you started in your business. However, a well-thought out strategic plan is extremely important to your success. Furthermore, execution upon your plan becomes even more important.

THE WIG

The final area this journal will help you get clarity is your WILDLY IM-PORTANT GOAL.

Most of us have a WIG but we are not clear on it. We also don't have the "what or why" questions answered. Moreover, the WIG is usually the goal that is pushing on you the most to execute. **Most of us have several goals in mind that we would like to achieve, however, the WIG is the one that usually takes up the most mental space dreaming about it.**

It's important to still pursue and create the roadmap to achieve your other goals, but the WIG is more urgent and, in some cases, feels unattainable because it is so big.

So, here's a way to begin working toward your "Why".

- What is your purpose for being?
- What can you begin working toward to live with more fulfillment?
- What were you put on this earth to create?

Now you can define this Wildly Important Goal and begin tracking your progress in this area.

HOW TO USE THIS JOURNAL

You will determine your **GOALS or OBJECTIVES based upon the answers of your "WHAT" and "WHY"**. But, in order to make drastic changes in the six areas of your life, you need to have a written plan with not only goals, but daily tactics that will get you there.

Goals are nothing without daily tactics. Without daily tactics, goals are simply dreams that we want to accomplish, but do not have a map of how to get there. **The daily tactics are the "HOW."** They are the roadmap and daily execution to achieving what we want.

For each of the six dimensions, you will answer the same questions as above:

> **Your Objective/Goal:**
> * *What* do I want to do?
> * *Why* do I want to do it?
>
> **Your Tactics:**
> * *How* will you do it?
> * *When* will you do it?

The "what and why" are the key drivers behind your goals. The "how and when" become the roadmap to achieving them.

Most of us don't get past the "what." We know what we want however, we don't usually explore the "why." The "why" is extremely important because it allows us to "gut check" our goals and truly explore if our goals are in-line with vision of our lives. If our "why" lines up with the vision for our lives, we are good to then ask ourselves the "how and when."

Again, "how and when" become the roadmap to our daily success, milestones, and tracking.

Without a way to measure our milestones, daily behaviors, and tactics goals will usually never be achieved.

ACCOUNTABILITY

The Dad Edge Alliance Community is committed to helping you become accountable, so you can achieve your goals.

We will help you create the roadmap, however, there is work YOU are responsible for.

- You need to **get clear on WHAT you want and WHY** you want it. If you are not clear on these two things, speak up, ask, and explore with someone else or within a call team.

- **Ask for feedback on your "what and why."** Allow others within the Alliance to challenge your thinking. This will help you truly vet out your goals and be able to look at them from other perspectives.

- Become clear on your "how and when." Again, your goals are just dreams in the distance without these 2 key elements. **Allow others within the Alliance to help you gut check your map.** This is important because you have to truly understand if your goals and tactics are: specific, measurable, attainable, relevant, and time sensitive (SMART GOAL).

- Accountability!! Accountability is critical. **Without an accountability partner, most of us will not execute.** In the Alliance, we have an entire community that will help you become accountable. HOWEVER, IT IS UP TO YOU TO PICK YOUR ACCOUNTABILITY PARTNER AND STRUCTURE YOUR SPECIFIC PLAN WITH THIS PARTNER. WE DO NOT ASSIGN YOU AN ACCOUNTABILITY PARTNER. We don't assign you an accountability partner for several reasons. There must be common goals with your partner. You must feel a certain amount of chemistry with this person.

LET'S DO THIS

Alright, we now have clarity on the six dimensions of our lives, the questions we need to ask ourselves to get clarity, and the roadmap for success.

Now it's time to take action!

On the following pages, this tracker will give you a clear roadmap to success and daily tactics you measure and give yourself a weekly score. We have given you the questions, the map, and the community to execute, however, it is up to you to execute.

DEFINING YOUR OBJECTIVES AND TACTICS

YOUR HEALTH:

Picture yourself 60 days from now. How do you want to look and feel physically, mentally, and spiritually?

Physically → Weight 175# → Lose Back Fat   225# Bench Press

Mentally → More Focused on 360 Man Project + Building Podcast

Spiritually → Growing Stronger → Reliant on God

WHAT ARE YOUR OBJECTIVES:

225# Bench Press

More Intent Focused, Vigilant, Mindful and Aware of who I am

Better + Closer Relationship with God

WHY ARE YOU STRIVING FOR THESE OBJECTIVES:

YOUR HEALTH: CONT'D

On the previous page you determined your health objective(s) "what" and "why." Now, use this Tactic page to determine "**how**" and "**when**" you will implement your objective(s).

Tactic 1

HOW:

WHEN:

Tactic 2 optional

HOW:

WHEN:

YOUR FINANCES:

Picture your financial situation 60 days from now. What changes will you make regarding your debt, income, savings and investments?

....
....
....
....

WHAT ARE YOUR OBJECTIVES:

....
....
....
....
....
....

WHY ARE YOU STRIVING FOR THESE OBJECTIVES:

....
....
....
....
....
....

YOUR FINANCES:

On the previous page you determined "what" and "why" of your financial objective(s). Now, use this Tactic page to determine "**how**" and "**when**" you will implement your objective(s).

Tactic 1

HOW:

WHEN:

Tactic 2 optional

HOW:

WHEN:

RELATIONSHIP WITH YOUR WIFE:

60 days from now, how do you picture your relationship with your wife?

....

....

....

....

WHAT ARE YOUR OBJECTIVES:

....

....

....

....

....

....

WHY ARE YOU STRIVING FOR THESE OBJECTIVES:

....

....

....

....

....

....

....

RELATIONSHIP WITH YOUR WIFE: CONT'D

On the previous page you determined "what" and "why" of your relationship objective(s). Now, use this Tactic page to determine "**how**" and "**when**" you will implement your objective(s).

Tactic 1

HOW:

....

....

....

....

....

....

WHEN:

....

....

....

Tactic 2 optional

HOW:

....

....

....

....

....

WHEN:

RELATIONSHIP WITH YOUR KIDS:

Picture yourself 60 days from now, how does your relationship with your kids feel? What new rituals and activities are you doing? How present and available do you want to be?

WHAT ARE YOUR OBJECTIVES:

WHY ARE YOU STRIVING FOR THESE OBJECTIVES:

RELATIONSHIP WITH YOUR KIDS: CONT'D

On the previous page you determined your objectives (s) you've set regarding your relationship with your children. Now, use this page to determine "**how**" and "**when**" you will implement your objective(s).

Tactic 1

HOW:

WHEN:

Tactic 2 optional

HOW:

WHEN:

YOUR BUSINESS:

Picture yourself 60 days from now. What is new and exciting about your business?

....

....

....

....

WHAT ARE YOUR OBJECTIVES:

....

....

....

....

....

....

WHY ARE YOU STRIVING FOR THESE OBJECTIVES:

....

....

....

....

....

....

....

....

YOUR BUSINESS: CONT'D

On the previous page you determined "what" and "why" of your business objective(s). Now, use this Tactic page to determine "**how**" and "**when**" you will implement your objective(s).

Tactic 1

HOW:

WHEN:

Tactic 2 optional

HOW:

WHEN:

WILDLY IMPORTANT GOALS:

Picture yourself 60 days from now. How much closer are you to accomplishing your wildly important goals? These are "wild" so no point in holding back!

WHAT ARE YOUR OBJECTIVES:

WHY ARE YOU STRIVING FOR THESE OBJECTIVES:

WILDLY IMPORTANT GOALS: CONT'D

On the previous page you determined "what" and "why" of your wildly important objective(s). Now, use this Tactic page to determine "**how**" and "**when**" you will implement your objective(s).

Tactic 1

HOW:

....

....

....

....

....

....

WHEN:

....

....

....

Tactic 2 optional

HOW:

....

....

....

....

....

WHEN:

It's time to start tracking your progress.

Now that you have written down your objectives and tactics on the previous pages, your next step will be to transfer them on to the tracker.

By coming back to the tracker **EVERYDAY for the next 13 weeks** you will begin to have more and more dominion over your life.

HEALTH OBJECTIVE:

1 Tactic:

2 Tactic: optional

RELATIONSHIP OBJECTIVE:

1 Tactic:

2 Tactic: optional

CHILDREN OBJECTIVE:

1 Tactic:

2 Tactic: optional

BUSINESS OBJECTIVE:

1 Tactic:

2 Tactic: optional

FINANCES OBJECTIVE:

1 Tactic:

2 Tactic: optional

W.I.G. OBJECTIVE:

1 Tactic:

2 Tactic: optional

DATE:

	MON	TUE	WED	THU	FRI	SAT	SUN	SCORE

	MON	TUE	WED	THU	FRI	SAT	SUN	SCORE

	MON	TUE	WED	THU	FRI	SAT	SUN	SCORE

	MON	TUE	WED	THU	FRI	SAT	SUN	SCORE

	MON	TUE	WED	THU	FRI	SAT	SUN	SCORE

	MON	TUE	WED	THU	FRI	SAT	SUN	SCORE

WEEKLY REFLECTION:

Reflect everyday on what's working with an emphasis on the positive aspects of your transformation. On this page reflect back on the six categories that you've set out to work on. Use the next page to reflect on your day to day progress.

HEALTH:
....
....
....

FINANCES:
....
....
....

RELATIONSHIP:
....
....
....

CHILDREN:
....
....
....

BUSINESS:
....
....
....

WILDLY IMPORTANT GOALS:
....
....
....
....

SUNDAY

MONDAY

TUESDAY

WEDNESDAY

THURSDAY

FRIDAY

SATURDAY

HEALTH OBJECTIVE:

1 Tactic:

2 Tactic: optional

RELATIONSHIP OBJECTIVE:

1 Tactic:

2 Tactic: optional

CHILDREN OBJECTIVE:

1 Tactic:

2 Tactic: optional

BUSINESS OBJECTIVE:

1 Tactic:

2 Tactic: optional

FINANCES OBJECTIVE:

1 Tactic:

2 Tactic: optional

W.I.G. OBJECTIVE:

1 Tactic:

2 Tactic: optional

DATE:

	MON	TUE	WED	THU	FRI	SAT	SUN	SCORE

	MON	TUE	WED	THU	FRI	SAT	SUN	SCORE

	MON	TUE	WED	THU	FRI	SAT	SUN	SCORE

	MON	TUE	WED	THU	FRI	SAT	SUN	SCORE

	MON	TUE	WED	THU	FRI	SAT	SUN	SCORE

	MON	TUE	WED	THU	FRI	SAT	SUN	SCORE

WEEKLY REFLECTION:

Reflect everyday on what's working with an emphasis on the positive aspects of your transformation. On this page reflect back on the six categories that you've set out to work on. Use the next page to reflect on your day to day progress.

HEALTH:

FINANCES:

RELATIONSHIP:

CHILDREN:

BUSINESS:

WILDLY IMPORTANT GOALS:

SUNDAY

MONDAY

TUESDAY

WEDNESDAY

THURSDAY

FRIDAY

SATURDAY

HEALTH OBJECTIVE:

1 Tactic:

2 Tactic: optional

RELATIONSHIP OBJECTIVE:

1 Tactic:

2 Tactic: optional

CHILDREN OBJECTIVE:

1 Tactic:

2 Tactic: optional

BUSINESS OBJECTIVE:

1 Tactic:

2 Tactic: optional

FINANCES OBJECTIVE:

1 Tactic:

2 Tactic: optional

W.I.G. OBJECTIVE:

1 Tactic:

2 Tactic: optional

DATE:

	MON	TUE	WED	THU	FRI	SAT	SUN	SCORE

	MON	TUE	WED	THU	FRI	SAT	SUN	SCORE

	MON	TUE	WED	THU	FRI	SAT	SUN	SCORE

	MON	TUE	WED	THU	FRI	SAT	SUN	SCORE

	MON	TUE	WED	THU	FRI	SAT	SUN	SCORE

	MON	TUE	WED	THU	FRI	SAT	SUN	SCORE

WEEKLY REFLECTION:

Reflect everyday on what's working with an emphasis on the positive aspects of your transformation. On this page reflect back on the six categories that you've set out to work on. Use the next page to reflect on your day to day progress.

HEALTH:

FINANCES:

RELATIONSHIP:

CHILDREN:

BUSINESS:

WILDLY IMPORTANT GOALS:

SUNDAY

MONDAY

TUESDAY

WEDNESDAY

THURSDAY

FRIDAY

SATURDAY

HEALTH OBJECTIVE:

1 Tactic:

2 Tactic: optional

RELATIONSHIP OBJECTIVE:

1 Tactic:

2 Tactic: optional

CHILDREN OBJECTIVE:

1 Tactic:

2 Tactic: optional

BUSINESS OBJECTIVE:

1 Tactic:

2 Tactic: optional

FINANCES OBJECTIVE:

1 Tactic:

2 Tactic: optional

W.I.G. OBJECTIVE:

1 Tactic:

2 Tactic: optional

DATE:

	MON	TUE	WED	THU	FRI	SAT	SUN	SCORE

	MON	TUE	WED	THU	FRI	SAT	SUN	SCORE

	MON	TUE	WED	THU	FRI	SAT	SUN	SCORE

	MON	TUE	WED	THU	FRI	SAT	SUN	SCORE

	MON	TUE	WED	THU	FRI	SAT	SUN	SCORE

	MON	TUE	WED	THU	FRI	SAT	SUN	SCORE

WEEKLY REFLECTION:

Reflect everyday on what's working with an emphasis on the positive aspects of your transformation. On this page reflect back on the six categories that you've set out to work on. Use the next page to reflect on your day to day progress.

HEALTH:

FINANCES:

RELATIONSHIP:

CHILDREN:

BUSINESS:

WILDLY IMPORTANT GOALS:

SUNDAY

MONDAY

TUESDAY

WEDNESDAY

THURSDAY

FRIDAY

SATURDAY

HEALTH OBJECTIVE:

1 Tactic:

2 Tactic: optional

RELATIONSHIP OBJECTIVE:

1 Tactic:

2 Tactic: optional

CHILDREN OBJECTIVE:

1 Tactic:

2 Tactic: optional

BUSINESS OBJECTIVE:

1 Tactic:

2 Tactic: optional

FINANCES OBJECTIVE:

1 Tactic:

2 Tactic: optional

W.I.G. OBJECTIVE:

1 Tactic:

2 Tactic: optional

DATE:

	MON	TUE	WED	THU	FRI	SAT	SUN	SCORE

	MON	TUE	WED	THU	FRI	SAT	SUN	SCORE

	MON	TUE	WED	THU	FRI	SAT	SUN	SCORE

	MON	TUE	WED	THU	FRI	SAT	SUN	SCORE

	MON	TUE	WED	THU	FRI	SAT	SUN	SCORE

	MON	TUE	WED	THU	FRI	SAT	SUN	SCORE

WEEKLY REFLECTION:

Reflect everyday on what's working with an emphasis on the positive aspects of your transformation. On this page reflect back on the six categories that you've set out to work on. Use the next page to reflect on your day to day progress.

HEALTH:

....

....

....

FINANCES:

....

....

....

RELATIONSHIP:

....

....

....

CHILDREN:

....

....

....

BUSINESS:

....

....

....

WILDLY IMPORTANT GOALS:

....

....

....

SUNDAY

MONDAY

TUESDAY

WEDNESDAY

THURSDAY

FRIDAY

SATURDAY

HEALTH OBJECTIVE:

1 Tactic:

2 Tactic: optional

RELATIONSHIP OBJECTIVE:

1 Tactic:

2 Tactic: optional

CHILDREN OBJECTIVE:

1 Tactic:

2 Tactic: optional

BUSINESS OBJECTIVE:

1 Tactic:

2 Tactic: optional

FINANCES OBJECTIVE:

1 Tactic:

2 Tactic: optional

W.I.G. OBJECTIVE:

1 Tactic:

2 Tactic: optional

DATE:

	MON	TUE	WED	THU	FRI	SAT	SUN	SCORE

	MON	TUE	WED	THU	FRI	SAT	SUN	SCORE

	MON	TUE	WED	THU	FRI	SAT	SUN	SCORE

	MON	TUE	WED	THU	FRI	SAT	SUN	SCORE

	MON	TUE	WED	THU	FRI	SAT	SUN	SCORE

	MON	TUE	WED	THU	FRI	SAT	SUN	SCORE

WEEKLY REFLECTION:

Reflect everyday on what's working with an emphasis on the positive aspects of your transformation. On this page reflect back on the six categories that you've set out to work on. Use the next page to reflect on your day to day progress.

HEALTH:

FINANCES:

RELATIONSHIP:

CHILDREN:

BUSINESS:

WILDLY IMPORTANT GOALS:

SUNDAY

MONDAY

TUESDAY

WEDNESDAY

THURSDAY

FRIDAY

SATURDAY

HEALTH OBJECTIVE:

1 Tactic:

2 Tactic:

RELATIONSHIP OBJECTIVE:

1 Tactic:

2 Tactic:

CHILDREN OBJECTIVE:

1 Tactic:

2 Tactic:

BUSINESS OBJECTIVE:

1 Tactic:

2 Tactic:

FINANCES OBJECTIVE:

1 Tactic:

2 Tactic:

W.I.G. OBJECTIVE:

1 Tactic:

2 Tactic:

DATE:

	MON	TUE	WED	THU	FRI	SAT	SUN	SCORE

	MON	TUE	WED	THU	FRI	SAT	SUN	SCORE

	MON	TUE	WED	THU	FRI	SAT	SUN	SCORE

	MON	TUE	WED	THU	FRI	SAT	SUN	SCORE

	MON	TUE	WED	THU	FRI	SAT	SUN	SCORE

	MON	TUE	WED	THU	FRI	SAT	SUN	SCORE

WEEKLY REFLECTION:

Reflect everyday on what's working with an emphasis on the positive aspects of your transformation. On this page reflect back on the six categories that you've set out to work on. Use the next page to reflect on your day to day progress.

HEALTH:

FINANCES:

RELATIONSHIP:

CHILDREN:

BUSINESS:

WILDLY IMPORTANT GOALS:

SUNDAY

MONDAY

TUESDAY

WEDNESDAY

THURSDAY

FRIDAY

SATURDAY

HEALTH OBJECTIVE:

1 Tactic:

2 Tactic:

RELATIONSHIP OBJECTIVE:

1 Tactic:

2 Tactic:

CHILDREN OBJECTIVE:

1 Tactic:

2 Tactic:

BUSINESS OBJECTIVE:

1 Tactic:

2 Tactic:

FINANCES OBJECTIVE:

1 Tactic:

2 Tactic:

W.I.G. OBJECTIVE:

1 Tactic:

2 Tactic:

DATE:

	MON	TUE	WED	THU	FRI	SAT	SUN	SCORE

	MON	TUE	WED	THU	FRI	SAT	SUN	SCORE

	MON	TUE	WED	THU	FRI	SAT	SUN	SCORE

	MON	TUE	WED	THU	FRI	SAT	SUN	SCORE

	MON	TUE	WED	THU	FRI	SAT	SUN	SCORE

	MON	TUE	WED	THU	FRI	SAT	SUN	SCORE

WEEKLY REFLECTION:

Reflect everyday on what's working with an emphasis on the positive aspects of your transformation. On this page reflect back on the six categories that you've set out to work on. Use the next page to reflect on your day to day progress.

HEALTH:

FINANCES:

RELATIONSHIP:

CHILDREN:

BUSINESS:

WILDLY IMPORTANT GOALS:

SUNDAY

MONDAY

TUESDAY

WEDNESDAY

THURSDAY

FRIDAY

SATURDAY

HEALTH OBJECTIVE:

1 Tactic:

2 Tactic:

RELATIONSHIP OBJECTIVE:

1 Tactic:

2 Tactic:

CHILDREN OBJECTIVE:

1 Tactic:

2 Tactic:

BUSINESS OBJECTIVE:

1 Tactic:

2 Tactic:

FINANCES OBJECTIVE:

1 Tactic:

2 Tactic:

W.I.G. OBJECTIVE:

1 Tactic:

2 Tactic:

DATE:

	MON	TUE	WED	THU	FRI	SAT	SUN	SCORE

	MON	TUE	WED	THU	FRI	SAT	SUN	SCORE

	MON	TUE	WED	THU	FRI	SAT	SUN	SCORE

	MON	TUE	WED	THU	FRI	SAT	SUN	SCORE

	MON	TUE	WED	THU	FRI	SAT	SUN	SCORE

	MON	TUE	WED	THU	FRI	SAT	SUN	SCORE

WEEKLY REFLECTION:

Reflect everyday on what's working with an emphasis on the positive aspects of your transformation. On this page reflect back on the six categories that you've set out to work on. Use the next page to reflect on your day to day progress.

HEALTH:

FINANCES:

RELATIONSHIP:

CHILDREN:

BUSINESS:

WILDLY IMPORTANT GOALS:

SUNDAY

MONDAY

TUESDAY

WEDNESDAY

THURSDAY

FRIDAY

SATURDAY

HEALTH OBJECTIVE:

1 Tactic:

2 Tactic:

RELATIONSHIP OBJECTIVE:

1 Tactic:

2 Tactic:

CHILDREN OBJECTIVE:

1 Tactic:

2 Tactic:

BUSINESS OBJECTIVE:

1 Tactic:

2 Tactic:

FINANCES OBJECTIVE:

1 Tactic:

2 Tactic:

W.I.G. OBJECTIVE:

1 Tactic:

2 Tactic:

DATE:

	MON	TUE	WED	THU	FRI	SAT	SUN	SCORE

	MON	TUE	WED	THU	FRI	SAT	SUN	SCORE

	MON	TUE	WED	THU	FRI	SAT	SUN	SCORE

	MON	TUE	WED	THU	FRI	SAT	SUN	SCORE

	MON	TUE	WED	THU	FRI	SAT	SUN	SCORE

	MON	TUE	WED	THU	FRI	SAT	SUN	SCORE

WEEKLY REFLECTION:

Reflect everyday on what's working with an emphasis on the positive aspects of your transformation. On this page reflect back on the six categories that you've set out to work on. Use the next page to reflect on your day to day progress.

HEALTH:

FINANCES:

RELATIONSHIP:

CHILDREN:

BUSINESS:

WILDLY IMPORTANT GOALS:

SUNDAY

MONDAY

TUESDAY

WEDNESDAY

THURSDAY

FRIDAY

SATURDAY

HEALTH OBJECTIVE:

1 Tactic:

2 Tactic:

RELATIONSHIP OBJECTIVE:

1 Tactic:

2 Tactic:

CHILDREN OBJECTIVE:

1 Tactic:

2 Tactic:

BUSINESS OBJECTIVE:

1 Tactic:

2 Tactic:

FINANCES OBJECTIVE:

1 Tactic:

2 Tactic:

W.I.G. OBJECTIVE:

1 Tactic:

2 Tactic:

DATE:

	MON	TUE	WED	THU	FRI	SAT	SUN	SCORE

	MON	TUE	WED	THU	FRI	SAT	SUN	SCORE

	MON	TUE	WED	THU	FRI	SAT	SUN	SCORE

	MON	TUE	WED	THU	FRI	SAT	SUN	SCORE

	MON	TUE	WED	THU	FRI	SAT	SUN	SCORE

	MON	TUE	WED	THU	FRI	SAT	SUN	SCORE

WEEKLY REFLECTION:

Reflect everyday on what's working with an emphasis on the positive aspects of your transformation. On this page reflect back on the six categories that you've set out to work on. Use the next page to reflect on your day to day progress.

HEALTH:

_____
_____
_____

FINANCES:

_____
_____
_____

RELATIONSHIP:

_____
_____
_____

CHILDREN:

_____
_____
_____

BUSINESS:

_____
_____
_____

WILDLY IMPORTANT GOALS:

_____
_____
_____

SUNDAY

MONDAY

TUESDAY

WEDNESDAY

THURSDAY

FRIDAY

SATURDAY

HEALTH OBJECTIVE:

1 Tactic:

2 Tactic:

RELATIONSHIP OBJECTIVE:

1 Tactic:

2 Tactic:

CHILDREN OBJECTIVE:

1 Tactic:

2 Tactic:

BUSINESS OBJECTIVE:

1 Tactic:

2 Tactic:

FINANCES OBJECTIVE:

1 Tactic:

2 Tactic:

W.I.G. OBJECTIVE:

1 Tactic:

2 Tactic:

DATE:

	MON	TUE	WED	THU	FRI	SAT	SUN	SCORE

	MON	TUE	WED	THU	FRI	SAT	SUN	SCORE

	MON	TUE	WED	THU	FRI	SAT	SUN	SCORE

	MON	TUE	WED	THU	FRI	SAT	SUN	SCORE

	MON	TUE	WED	THU	FRI	SAT	SUN	SCORE

	MON	TUE	WED	THU	FRI	SAT	SUN	SCORE

WEEKLY REFLECTION:

Reflect everyday on what's working with an emphasis on the positive aspects of your transformation. On this page reflect back on the six categories that you've set out to work on. Use the next page to reflect on your day to day progress.

HEALTH:

FINANCES:

RELATIONSHIP:

CHILDREN:

BUSINESS:

WILDLY IMPORTANT GOALS:

SUNDAY

MONDAY

TUESDAY

WEDNESDAY

THURSDAY

FRIDAY

SATURDAY

HEALTH OBJECTIVE:

1 Tactic:

2 Tactic:

RELATIONSHIP OBJECTIVE:

1 Tactic:

2 Tactic:

CHILDREN OBJECTIVE:

1 Tactic:

2 Tactic:

BUSINESS OBJECTIVE:

1 Tactic:

2 Tactic:

FINANCES OBJECTIVE:

1 Tactic:

2 Tactic:

W.I.G. OBJECTIVE:

1 Tactic:

2 Tactic:

DATE:

	MON	TUE	WED	THU	FRI	SAT	SUN	SCORE

	MON	TUE	WED	THU	FRI	SAT	SUN	SCORE

	MON	TUE	WED	THU	FRI	SAT	SUN	SCORE

	MON	TUE	WED	THU	FRI	SAT	SUN	SCORE

	MON	TUE	WED	THU	FRI	SAT	SUN	SCORE

	MON	TUE	WED	THU	FRI	SAT	SUN	SCORE

WEEKLY REFLECTION:

Reflect everyday on what's working with an emphasis on the positive aspects of your transformation. On this page reflect back on the six categories that you've set out to work on. Use the next page to reflect on your day to day progress.

HEALTH:

FINANCES:

RELATIONSHIP:

CHILDREN:

BUSINESS:

WILDLY IMPORTANT GOALS:

SUNDAY

MONDAY

TUESDAY

WEDNESDAY

THURSDAY

FRIDAY

SATURDAY

SCORING

		Week 1	Week 2	Week 3	Week 4	Week 5
HEALTH	Tactic 1:					
	Tactic 2:					
FINANCES	Tactic 1:					
	Tactic 2:					
RELATIONSHIP	Tactic 1:					
	Tactic 2:					
CHILDREN	Tactic 1:					
	Tactic 2:					
BUSINESS	Tactic 1:					
	Tactic 2:					
W.I.G.	Tactic 1:					
	Tactic 2:					
		Week 1	Week 2	Week 3	Week 4	Week 5
TOTALS:						

Week 6	Week 7	Week 8	Week 9	Week 10	Week 11	Week 12	Week 13

Week 6	Week 7	Week 8	Week 9	Week 10	Week 11	Week 12	Week 13

Change your objectives and tactics as you see fit to be sure
you're having success along this 13 week journey.

FINAL REFLECTION:

Use this page for reflecting back on where you began when you started the tracker and where you ended up by the end of this journal. What lessons did you learn? How does it feel? What was most moving about this process? What will you continue to work on? What and how would you like to celebrate?

If you have used all 13 weeks, congratulations!

You can order another Edge Tracker at
gooddadproject.com/product/edge-tracker/

For more information please visit GoodDadProject.com.

Written by Larry Hagner, GoodDadProject.com

Design by Perry Towle, Ungloo.com **ungloo**

28240486R00052

Made in the USA
Lexington, KY
11 January 2019